Gallopade Publishing Group Presents . . .

Virginia Law for Kids!:
"Make It, Don't Break It"

by Carole Marsh
©Copyright Carole Marsh

What is **"copyright law"**? It is the legal protection of original material created by an artist. This might be a children's book, a cartoon, a rock song, or a photograph. It might be a *patent* for a unique new item or process. Or it could be a *trademarked* name, like Mickey Mouse. If you *illegally* photocopy or reproduce copyrighted material, you have *infringed* on the rights of its creator, the copyright holder. This can result in legal action, such as being taken to court, or sued. If you are found guilty, you might be fined, or put in jail. If you get *permission* to use the copyrighted material that's ok.
It pays to KNOW THE LAW

This book has material which correlates with the Virginia Standards of Learning. At every opportunity, we have tried to coordinate information with the Social Sciences and History, English, Science and Math, Civics, Economics, and Computer Technology SOL directives for grades 3-12. For additional information, go to our websites: www.virginiaexperience.com or www.gallopade.com.!

📖 Other Books by Carole Marsh

Virginia History: Surprising Secrets About Our State's Founding Mothers, Fathers, & Kids!

Virginia Indians: A Kid's Look at Our State's Chiefs, Tribes, Reservations, Powwows, Lore & More From the Past & the Present

Virginia Government for Kids: The Cornerstone of Everyday Life in Our State!

My First Book About Virginia!

Virginia "Jeopardy!": Answers & Questions About Our State

Virginia "Jography!": A Fun Run Thru Our State

Virginia Timelines!: A Chronology of Virginia History, Mystery, Trivia, Legend, Lore & More

Virginia Jurassic Park!: Dinosaurs & Other Prehistoric Creatures That Once Roamed Our State

Virginia State Greats!

"Avast Ye Slobs!": Virginia Pirates & Treasure Trivia

Virginia Silly Trivia!

Virginia Book-in-a-Bag Reproducible Activities!

Virginia Facts & Factivities,
an interactive multimedia CD-ROM
+
Carole Marsh Mysteries
&
The Big Instruction Book of Small Business,
Virginia Edition

Table of Contents

A Word From the Author 4
From Cradle to Grave! 5
What is Virginia Law, Anyway? 6
Virginia Law Comes in Many Flavors! 7
The Law of the Land! 8
Everyday Virginia Law! 9
Funny Old Virginia Laws! 10
The Legislative Branch of the Virginia Tree 11
Local Law Versus State Law 12
Laws Can Change Your World! 13
How Laws Are Passed in Virginia 14
Armchair Law, or Why NOT to be a Lazy Citizen! 15
Breaking the Law! 16
Old Time Punishments for Breaking the Law 17
Can Kids Break Virginia Laws? 18
Well, Gee! Don't Virginia Kids Have Any Rights? 19
The Law of Our Virginia Land! 20
It's Just Plain Criminal! 21
A Jury of Your Peers? 22
Order in the Court! 23
Virginia Trial of the Century! 24
Virginia Trial of the Century Warm Up 24
Law Trivia You Should Know! 26
Legal Morals & Ethics 27
Appendix: Legal Careers 28
Other Legal Opportunities! 29
A Glossary of Plain English Legal Terms 30
A Glossary of Foreign Legal Terms, in Plain English! 33
Bibliography 34
About the Author 35
Index 36

📖 A Legal Word From the Author!

Dear Kids,

I specialize in writing books for kids, and no matter what the subject (even "the law"), I try to make it fascinating, factual, and funny!

When I hear the word LAW, I always think of that silly poem: *Order in the court/The judge has gotta spit/Who can't swim/Better git!* . . . or the saying that goes, "Better your head in the mouth of a lion than in the hands of an attorney" . . . or "spaghetti westerns" where guys in long black coats took the law in their own hands in early frontier America. I even remember when my father, a former county marshal, would serve as court bailiff, crying out, "Oh yea, oh yea, oh yea, oh yea" before the judge entered the room (while I sat in the back of the courtroom giggling!)

But Virginia law has a much more serious side, and it isn't one bit boring. Today, when we have a lot of "youthful offenders" (kids who get in trouble with the law), our state law is not a laughing matter.

Think about it: Virginia law affects everyone, even kids, in our state every single day! So when should you begin to learn about our state legal and legislative systems? Right now is a great time!

In this book, you'll read some funny old laws still on the books. You'll learn the facts behind some of that law stuff you see on television. You'll read about briefs that aren't underwear! But most importantly, you'll enjoy learning why we have state laws, what they have to do with you, and your (yes, I said YOUR!) role in the amazing legal process that works to the benefit of each and every Virginia citizen — no matter what their age.

Carole Marsh

From Cradle to Grave!

What is VIRGINIA LAW? It is all the ideas, rules, and legal codes that govern the citizens of Virginia. Our state has certain powers; it uses laws to enforce them.

YOU are part of this legal process from the time you are born (gotta have a birth certificate; it's a law) until the time you die (gotta have a death certificate; it's a law), and all times in between. Whether you get married, start a business, rob a bank, or almost anything else good or bad, you will find yourself on one side of Virginia law, or another.

There are all kinds of law: civil law and common law; constitutional law and commercial law; maritime law and military law. Some laws are very simple and easy to abide by. Other laws and legal matters are more snarled than a cat in grandpa's fishing line! Some laws are so silly that they should have been shoved off the books long ago. And the law is always controversial — if you think people don't agree about the weather, well just ask them about the law!

The truth is we find Virginia law exciting, or else why would murder trials and criminals turn up on headline news almost every night? But we also find it boring: ever had to stand in line while Mom waited to get her driver's license renewed? Yawn!

Virginia law is about Big Books filled with Big Words that "look like Greek to me" (actually, they're Latin!). But Virginia law is more about people: the people who live happily because of the law; the folks who enforce the law; the baddies who break the law; and, the people who are responsible for thinking hard about Virginia law and how it can best meet the needs of citizens of all ages. This means YOU!

What is Virginia Law, Anyway?

One way to think about what law is . . . is to think about the lawless life. What if our state had no laws? What would life be like? How would people act? If you can imagine this, then you can also easily imagine why we need law and what law is: a system to help people live together in harmony, even when they disagree.

Just like everything else in our state, Virginia law has a history. The "common law" we enjoy as citizens dates back to England. When early colonists came to America, they brought their ideas of the law along with them. The original states even used decisions made under English law to guide them in deciding how to handle disputes that arose in their new home in the New World.

But as the United States grew, each state also passed its own laws that helped them to manage the affairs of their citizens. So, you could say that Virginia law is a combination of 2 things:

1. **Legal precedents** — We are eager to uphold laws already on the books unless new information or circumstances convinces us that there needs to be a change in the law.

2. **Legislation** — Virginia legislators originate, debate, and pass (or reject) new laws that help our state keep up with the legal times.

Virginia law is important for many reasons. After all, a law passed in Virginia could cause similar laws to be changed around America!

NAME 1 FAMOUS VIRGINIA JURIST: _____

Virginia Law Comes in Many Flavors!

Here is a matching quiz for you to see just a few of the many kinds of laws it takes to run our state. See how well you do! (The answers are in small type at the bottom of the page, so don't peek.)

If I am this, I might use what type of law?

1. Bank robber
2. Business person
3. State park
4. Virginia
5. Hospital
6. Real estate agent
7. Corporation
8. Ship owner
9. Diplomat
10. Soldier

Laws of many types

A. Military Law
B. International Law
C. Constitutional Law
D. Medical Law
E. Maritime Law
F. Commercial Law
G. Criminal Law
H. Property Law
I. Antitrust Law
J. Environmental Law

Answers: 1-G; 2-F; 3-J; 4-C; 5-D; 6-H ; 7-I; 8-E; 9-B; 10-A

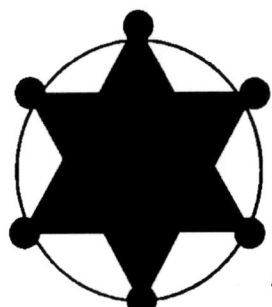

The Law of the Land!

Why do we need laws in Virginia? If we live in a democracy, or free country, why can't we each do exactly what we please?

Well, I'm sure you know this is a silly question! Can't you just picture busy roads without traffic signals, banks with no doors, schools with no rules, and work places with no leaders, guidelines, or even clocks?

Laws are just common sense rules that help people live together in the best way. Our state government makes laws to help people:

-Be safe.
-Be treated fairly.
-Do their jobs.
-Act properly in public.

Even laws are not set in stone forever. Some very old laws on the books such as, "It is illegal to sneeze on a train," are silly today, even if there might once have been a very good reason for them. Some laws become outdated, such as those regarding hitching your horse to a post in town.

New times and situations call for new laws. The people bring up ideas for these new rules. Our state government enacts these laws. People uphold these laws as long as they are in force. What happens to people who break the law? They are punished — *according to the law.*

Everyday Virginia Law!

Here are some activities to help you think about how much the laws in our state affect your life each and every day.

Make a list of 3 Virginia laws that affect you. (Think of traffic laws, shoplifting laws, landlord/tenant laws, real estate laws, laws regarding contracts, getting paid at work, etc., marriage laws, divorce laws, adoption laws, criminal law, and many others!)

1._____
2._____
3._____

What new Virginia law would you enact if you could?:
_____
Why would you pass this law?:
_____

What Virginia law would you *repeal* (get rid of) if you could?:
_____
Why would you repeal this law?:
_____

The attorney general of Virginia is the head legal person in our state. **Who is our state's attorney general?:**
_____

Your local legislator (elected representative) is the key person that tries to ensure that the laws that affect you are good ones. **Who is your local legislator?:**
_____

Funny Old Virginia Laws!

Here is a funny quiz for you! On the left side is an old Virginia law. Surely there was once a good reason for it? You decide what that might be and write it to the right of the law. (It's always a good idea to stay on the right side of the law!)

LAW	PURPOSE OF LAW
NO HUNTING ON MAIN STREET!	_____
NO PLAYING MARBLES FOR KEEPS!	_____
YOU MUST GET A DOCTOR'S PRESCRIPTION BEFORE YOU TAKE A BATH!	_____
YOU CAN'T OWN A CAT AND A BIRD AT THE SAME TIME!	_____
WOMEN'S DRESSES CAN'T BE MORE THAN 2 INCHES ABOVE THE ANKLE!	_____
A MAN CANNOT MARRY HIS WIFE'S GRANDMOTHER!	_____
NO WORKING IN BARE FEET!	_____
A DEAD PERSON CANNOT SERVE ON A JURY!	_____
YOU CANNOT SLEEP IN SOMEONE'S OUTHOUSE WITHOUT PERMISSION!	_____

The Legislative Branch of the Virginia Tree

Our state government is like our federal, or U.S., government, in many ways:

-Virginia has a state constitution.
-Virginia has a legislative branch of government to enact laws.
-Virginia has a law enforcement branch to enforce laws.

Virginia has some unique things about its governmental set-up. These include:

-Our state is a Commonwealth
-Our state Capitol has a House of Delegates
-Our state's counties have a Board of Supervisors

This all means that the people are supposed to run the government, and not the other way around! The people have to abide by the laws that are enacted by the people, BUT, if they want to change the laws or the state constitution, they can do so.

OH, so you didn't know you had so much power? Well, of course you do! Virginia is your state. And outside of reading about the legal matters of the state, the best way to learn more is to get involved in the process. Here are a few ways. Put a checkmark by those that would be good for you to do, and an X by those that would not!

__Visit a court while it is in session
__Sign a petition to say you want a law changed or added
__Participate in a debate about a new or changed law
__Break a law to see what happens
__Take a tour of the state legislature
__Meet your local legislator
__Participate in a "Kangaroo Court" mock trial

SPEAK EASY Local Law Vs. State Law

State law is not just about what happens in the Virginia legislature while it is in session and passing laws. Lawmaking (and breaking!) is going on right out your own back door in your city, town, or county. What happens on all these levels affects the everyday life of you, your parents, your school, your job, and every other aspect of life. Check which level you think applies to the everyday legal matters below:

LEGAL MATTER	**State/County/City,Town**
You are born-need a birth certificate!	____/____/_____
Have to get a measles shot before you can enter school!	____/____/_____
At last, you're old enough to drive, but must get a driver's license!	____/____/_____
Ah, love! Getting married, hey? Supposed to get a blood test first!	____/____/_____
Hey, it's time to vote! Registration required!	____/____/_____
Buying your first house? Sign on the dotted line in the contract, please!	____/____/_____
Gonna start your own business? Want to be open on Sunday? Well, what do the "blue laws" say?	____/____/_____

 Laws Can Change Your World!

"But I hear people complain about the law!" you say. Well, that's true. Of course, many times people are just complaining, when they really understand the need and purpose of the law. Other times, they may think that some laws are unfair, outdated, oppressive, or, even too liberal and not strict enough. It's no wonder that Virginia "Law Land" is a busy place!

If you want to see how important laws are to us, just look back in time and see if you would like any of these laws to go back to the way they once were! Our state and local laws change with the times, because the times change and people want the laws changed too. Complaining doesn't accomplish anything.

Carole's "Believe-It-Or-Not!" — Laws of the Past
Check the ones YOU are glad were changed!

❏ Women and Blacks do not have the right to vote, even if they are American citizens.

❏ "Robber Barrons" can operate a monopoly so that others cannot have a chance to compete, even if people do lose their jobs or make terribly low wages for very, very long hours.

❏ Child labor (meaning very young children) working long, long hours in poor conditions for pennies in pay is legal.

❏ It is ok to own slaves, to work them as hard as you wish, to buy and sell them, even if that divides families so that they never see one another again.

How Laws Are Passed in Virginia

How about a simple explanation of how we get new laws in our state? Here goes:

1. Your parents discuss some ideas over dinner. You are listening. "I think that would be a good law!" you insist.

2. While you may not know it, other people in your community are thinking the same thing. They begin to talk to one another over the backyard fence, at the grocery store, and at work. Your Mom says, "I think I'll call our local representative and tell her what I think."

3. Newspaper articles and tv and radio broadcasts often discuss the changes that you have been hearing about. One day, on the way to school, you actually hear your local representative say on the radio, "I plan to submit this bill during the next legislative session."

4. Sure enough, months go by, but one day the headline on your newspaper says, *Bill Submitted-What Do the People Want?*

5. More time goes by. The bill outlining the proposed new law has been introduced in the legislature. It goes to a committee for review and discussion. One day, the bill is debated by all the legislators.

6. No one can agree what to do; the bill is sent back to the committee for some changes. At last, it comes back to the floor of the legislature.

7. A vote is taken — the bill is passed!

8. The approved bill is signed into law by the governor.

You asked for it — you got it! That's the way the law works!!

TIME'S RUNNING OUT... Armchair Law, or, Why NOT to Be a Lazy Citizen!

You are excited! An idea that was discussed at your very kitchen table and in your classroom is now a new Virginia law. Maybe you were in favor of this law; perhaps you were very much against it. So, did you do anything? Well, why not!

What can you, even a kid, do to help get the laws that you believe are needed in our state. Here are a few ideas. Put a ✔ by the ones you think you'd like to try.

THINGS I CAN DO TO IMPROVE VIRGINIA LAWS!

❏ I can listen and read about proposed laws. I can ask questions about things I don't understand.

❏ Once I form my opinion, I can share it with others. Who knows, they might even listen to me!

❏ I can write my representatives and tell them what I think. If I can't find their names and addresses in my current phone book, I can ask my librarian — she's always helpful!

❏ If I belong to a club or group of people (like the Girl Scouts or Boy Scouts, for example), I can bring up the matter with them. Maybe we can state as a group that we are for or against the proposed law. There's power in numbers, I've heard!

❏ I can take a petition around and get people to sign it. If I can get enough people to agree, I can send it to legislators — surely this will influence them?

❏ I can organize and/or participate in a peaceful demonstration. How will people know what I think if I don't make some noise?

Breaking the Law!

We hear a lot about crime in Virginia. Crime comes in all "flavors." Some crimes are petty, but they are crimes because someone did not follow the rules. Some crimes are pretty awful, such as murder. Like a parent, the government's job is to try to make the punishment fit the crime.

When an adult breaks the law, different things happen, depending on the rule broken. If a person parks too long at a parking meter, they may just get a parking ticket. They also have the choice to go to court to fight this punishment, if they think it is unfair. For example, if the parking meter was broken and they couldn't get their money in it, they may not feel that they broke the law.

If an adult commits a serious crime, he or she may be arrested and have to appear in court to explain the situation. If there is enough evidence that the person truly did commit the crime, then they may have a trial in a court of law.

Even a person who does something really bad has laws to protect them. They are entitled to have a lawyer represent them. If they can't afford to pay a lawyer, a lawyer will be appointed to represent them for free.

As you can see, Virginia government creates laws to protect all the people. This is called their "constitutional right" because the main law of our land, the *U.S. Constitution* says that's the way it will be!

QUESTION: WHAT CONSTITUTIONAL RIGHT DO YOU VALUE THE MOST?:_____

Old Time Punishments for Breaking the Law

Let's face it: one of the smartest things you can ever do in life is not break the law! But some old time punishments seem like greater deterrents to breaking the law than an air-conditioned cell with a television. See what you think! Try to match the punishment with its explanation. Ouch!

PUNISHMENT   **EXPLANATION**

1. Ducking Stool   A. Chopping off your head

2. Scold's Bridle   B. Arms & legs tied to horses which run and pull you apart

3. Pillory   C. Being enclosed in a case of spikes

4. Jougs   D. Forced to march around in a barrel

5. Stocks   E. Being mashed to death

6. Drunkard's Cloak   F. Mask of spikes worn over the face

7. Draw & Quarter   G. Dunked into water until you almost drown

8. *Peine forte et dure*   H. Clamped by the head & hands in public

9. Iron Maiden   I. Being chained in public while people tease you

10. Decapitation   J. Hung from an iron collar & whipped

Answer: 1-G; 2-F; 3-H; 4-J; 5-I; 6-D; 7-B; 8-E; 9-C; 10-A

Can Kids Break Virginia Laws?

Oops! Unfortunately, they do it all the time. It is not a very good idea. If you really want to value the freedom you have under our democratic government, just spend some time sitting in a *reformatory*, or jail for kids. On second thought, just take my word for it! It's a beautiful sunny day in Virginia and you want to be outdoors, not locked up behind bars.

What is a kid? According to Virginia state law, anyone under the age of 18-years-old, is a *minor* or child. If you break a law as a child, you may have to appear in *juvenile court*. You may be put on *probation*, which means that you have to follow certain rules to help keep you from breaking the law again. You may be placed in a foster home if the judge thinks that this is the best idea. Or, you might be sent to a reformatory.

Most people go through their entire lives without breaking the law. Some people break the law once, but realize that this is not the best thing to do and never break another law. Some people seem to be in trouble with "the law" all the time. ***The choice is yours.*** One of our state government's most important jobs is to protect law-abiding citizens.

QUESTION: SHOULD CHILDREN BE TRIED AS ADULTS? THIS IS A CONTROVERSIAL ISSUE IN OUR STATE AND AMERICA TODAY. SEE WHAT YOU CAN FIND OUT ABOUT IT.

Well, Gee! Don't Virginia Kids Have Any Rights?

In the United States, children do not have all the rights that adults do. (Of course, you will when you turn 18!) That's why you don't see 6-year-olds driving cars or 12-year-olds voting.

But kids do have many rights. Just a few of these include the right to:

-Be protected by laws
-Have a name
-Have a country to be a citizen of
-Be taken care of by their parents
-Get an education

American children also have many of the same rights as adults. The law says that you can belong to any religion you choose. You can say anything you want to (although I'm not sure I'd try that with your Dad!) You can write almost anything you want to (the "Freedom of Speech" law covers this) even if what you write is dumb or mean.

In many countries, kids do not have these basic rights that children in America may even take for granted. One of the main jobs of Virginia government is to work hard to be sure that children, from the time even before they are born, are protected by law from anything that could keep them from growing up in a healthy, normal way.

American kids are the luckiest kids in the world!

The Law of Our Virginia Land!

Our state and local laws are just words written on paper. They would be useless without the people and the systems that make the laws work (not to mention the good citizens who obey them, like you!)

Here are just a few of the people and places that enforce and interpret Virginia law:

State Supreme Court: This is the Queen Bee of our state court system. This is the place landmark court cases may take place. Those people in the long, black robes — they're the *judges* and they're in charge.

Court of Appeals: In many cases, you can "appeal" the verdict in a court case and go back to court. Sounds like you're going round and round? That's right, but it's your right. *Justice* is what you are after.

Courts, Courts, Courts: Additional courts in the state may include county court, district court, circuit court, municipal court, probate court, police court, juvenile court, family court, tax court, and many others.

But what would courts do without:

Police, Sheriffs and others who try to enforce the laws.

Lawyers (also called attorneys) who practice the law by helping people with their legal matters for a fee. If you can't afford a lawyer, one may be appointed by the court for you for free.

And then there are the reporters who cover court for their newspapers, magazines or television stations, law schools that educate people to become lawyers, law reviews that write about the law, and many other legal-schmegal folks!

It's Just Plain Criminal!

Probably no aspect of Virginia law is more interesting to people of all ages than a jury trial. Since kids have big imaginations, I'm sure it is easy for you to imagine yourself as the defendant in a trial that may even be covered live on television. What if you're innocent? WHAT IF YOU'RE GUILTY?!

Trial of the Century!

To learn more about a criminal jury trial, I have a great activity planned for you! If you fill-in the information requested as we go along on the next few pages, you will be ready to write an original courtroom drama. Use your imagination as well as things you have read or heard about. Perhaps you can re-enact your jury trial in front of the class?

The Cast of Characters
GIVE A FICTIONAL NAME to the people who will serve in these roles for your Virginia Trial of the Century!:

Judge _____-In charge of the trial. He or she sits on a platform called the bench. Stand when the judge enters; be quiet if the gavel is rapped!

The **Defendant** _____-This is the person accused of having committed a crime. Remember, she or he is innocent until proven guilty!

The **Defense Attorney** _____-A lawyer who will try to get the defendant found "not guilty" by the jury.

The **Prosecuting Attorney** _____-The lawyer who will try to convict the defendant of the crime.

The Jury-12 people who decide whether the defendant is guilty or innocent. List their names on the next page.

A Jury of Your Peers?

Talk about peer pressure! The people who are really in charge of this Virginia Trial of the Century are the 12 members of the jury. Fill out the information requested about them below:

Jury No.	**Age**	**Occupation**
1. _____	_____	_____
2. _____	_____	_____
3. _____	_____	_____
4. _____	_____	_____
5. _____	_____	_____
6. _____	_____	_____
7. _____	_____	_____
8. _____	_____	_____
9. _____	_____	_____
10. _____	_____	_____
11. _____	_____	_____
12. _____	_____	_____

And 2 alternate jurors, in case the regular jurors can no longer serve on account of illness or some other reason:

13. _____	_____	_____
14. _____	_____	_____

Order in the Court!

Establish the setting for your Virginia Trial of the Century by filling in the blanks below:

The trial will be held in Courtroom 101 at the courthouse in our capital city of: _____.

The defendant is _____ years old and is charged with the crime of_____. He/she will plead: __Guilty/__Not Guilty.

Items to be entered into evidence during the trial include:
1._____
2._____
3._____
4._____
5._____
6._____

Witnesses for the *prosecution* include (give type of person: doctor, police officer, etc.):
A._____ B._____
C._____ D._____

Witnesses for the *defense* include:
A._____ B._____
C._____ D._____

On a separate sheet of paper, draw a sketch of your courtroom. Be sure and include:
The judge at the bench
The jury in the jury box
The prosecuting lawyers at their table
The defendant & his/her lawyers at their table
The bailiff, who will swear in the witnesses
The clerk of court who will keep the official record
The witness stand, and the witnesses in the courtroom

©Carole Marsh/Gallopade International/800-536-2GET/www.gallopade.com/Page 23

Virginia Trial of the Century!

Each trial has a beginning, a middle, and an ending. Here is a brief description of what will happen in general at your make-believe trial. Use this information to expand your story in a notebook or on your computer. Perhaps you'd like to turn it into a play that can be performed in class? If so, you might want to pay attention to *dialogue*, or what people actually say during the trial. (If you want to use some real "law" words, see the glossary in this book!)

THE BEGINNING: The jury is instructed by the judge that they are here to serve justice by listening to the evidence, and then making a decision about whether the defendant is innocent or guilty. The lawyers make their *opening statements* to try to convince you that the person charged with the crime is innocent or guilty.

THE MIDDLE: Witnesses are called and sworn to tell "the truth, the whole truth, and nothing but the truth." If they lie *under oath*, they *perjure* themselves, and may be held in *contempt of court*. (This means that they could end up going to jail themselves!) The prosecution calls its witnesses first and gives them a *direct examination* by asking them questions. The defense lawyer then gets to *cross-examine* the witness, asking more questions. Next, the defense calls its witnesses, and the same process occurs. During these examinations of witnesses, either side can *introduce evidence* into the court.

THE END: Once both sides "rest their case", each side's lawyer gives a *final summation*. This is usually a very dramatic, emotional speech where one lawyer tries to convince the jury that the defendant is guilty, while the other lawyer assures the jury that the defendant is innocent. The judge then *charges the jury*, giving them specific instructions about what they are to do. They then go to the jury room where they *deliberate* (consider) all the evidence they have heard. Once they decide on a *verdict*, they let the judge know. (If they can't reach a verdict, the jury is *deadlocked*. The judge may send the jury back to try once more to reach a verdict. If they still can't, it is a *hung jury*. In this event, the charges may be dropped or there may be another trial.) Everyone returns to the courtroom and the verdict is read. Be prepared for smiles of relief . . . or tears of despair! And, be prepared for an *appeal* of the verdict . . . another trial, and, another jury.

Hear Ye! Virginia Trial of the Century Warm Up!

To help you get ready to write your dramatic "Virginia Trial of the Century", take some time to research and find out what the most famous trial in our state has been so far!

Most Famous Virginia Trial:_____
vs_____

Year the trial began:_____

Year the trial ended:_____

Who was on trial?:_____

What were they accused of?_____

Give a brief synopsis of the trial:
_____
_____
_____
_____
_____
_____
_____

What was the verdict?:_____

How did this verdict change Virginia legal history?:
_____
_____
_____
_____
_____
_____

Law Trivia You Should Know!

Who's Miranda?: You see this legal right on tv all the time! It's when the arresting officer says, "You have the right to remain silent", etc. A person is "Mirandized" so that they have legally been told their rights, including that they don't have to speak at that time, but that if they do, it could be used against them, and, that if they can't afford a lawyer, the court will appoint one for them.

Taking the Fifth!: What does it mean when you hear someone on trial say, "I take the fifth"? They are referring to the Fifth Amendment of the Constitution which says that a person is not required to give testimony which will incriminate (prove) that they are guilty of a crime. Of course, that doesn't mean that other witnesses can't tell all!

Have You Ever Seen a Lawyer's Briefs?: No, I don't mean undercover underwear! A legal *brief* is a written summary of information that will be involved in a trial. It is *filed* (shared with others) before a trial begins.

Legal-Schmegal: "Why are legal contracts so very, very looooooong and so full of weird words and complicated sentences?" Good question! Let's face it, most legal writers would flunk your English class. In some ways, written law is complex because legal matters are complicated. Lawyers want to "dot every i and cross every t" (that means they want to cover all their legal bases.) On the other hand, if things are written in such a snarled manner then maybe later, a lawyer can get someone out of a contract by untangling the language it is written in to suit themselves. Fortunately today, some legal documents are being written in plain English. This is fair and saves everyone a lot of time and headaches!

What is that little *v* or *vs* for?: That stands for *versus*, as in against. So, Roe v. Wade = Roe versus Wade.

Legal Morals & Ethics

There is a secret to what makes "the law" work successfully in Virginia. That secret is *obedience*! Most people go through their entire lives without breaking the law. They may not really even think about it; they just know that living within the law is the only way people can remain civilized and live together in harmony.

While this might sound easy, it's surprising how tempting it can be to break the law. Sometimes, you can even break the law without knowing it. But have you ever heard the phrase, "Ignorance is no excuse of the law." That's true!

Test your legal morals and ethics on the quiz below. Don't look for answers at the end — only <u>you</u> can say how you would react!

I. You get a good job and make a lot of money one year. If you report it all on your income tax form, you will have to pay more money. If you don't report it all, you will get a refund.
I WOULD: __REPORT IT ALL/__NOT REPORT IT ALL

II. You witness a serious traffic accident. The person who caused the accident promises to write you a check for $1,000 if you will just leave and not be a witness.
I WOULD: __LEAVE WITH THE CHECK/__STAY TILL THE POLICE COMES AND TELL WHAT I SAW

III. You get called to jury duty. While you would like to serve, you are really busy. Besides, you don't want to risk missing any of your vacation.
__I LIE TO THE JUDGE AND TELL HER MY MOTHER IS DYING/__I TELL THE JUDGE THE TRUTH, EVEN IF IT MEANS I END UP SERVING ON THE JURY

IV. You serve on a jury. All the other jury members vote guilty, but you think the defendant is innocent. YOU:__CHANGE YOUR MIND/__STICK TO YOUR GUNS

Appendix: Legal Careers

So you want to be a lawyer? Or a *paralegal*, who assists lawyers? Or have another career in some aspect related to the law? What do you do next? Well, for starters, study hard! Every subject you're taking in school might come in handy some day if you are involved in The Law!

Here are some other ways you can begin to prepare for a legal career: Learn to write and speak well — this is how lawyers communicate. Good typing skills are a plus if you want your computer keyboard to fly while you are doing your legal writing. Perhaps you can get a summer job in a law office someday. Or sit in on a trial. Or visit the courthouse.

If you think you'd like to attend law school, consider studying political science or government. You might take the LSAT (Law School Aptitude Test). You will need 3 years of college before you can enroll in 3 years of law school. *Whew!*

If you graduate from law school, you will probably want to take the *bar exam*. Being "admitted to the bar" means you have passed this test and meet all the other requirements set by the Virginia Bar Association. Once you get your license to practice law, you can "hang out your shingle" (go into practice on your own) or go to work with a law firm or as a lawyer for a corporation.

Some lawyers are sort of like family doctors, they help people with day-to-day legal matters, such as preparing a will or contracting to buy a home. Other lawyers *specialize* in certain aspects of the law. Examples include civil rights law, consumer protection, copyright law, labor law, and many others.

Some lawyers become *partners* in firms and generally make a lot of money. Many lawyers enjoy doing *pro bono* work, or practicing law for free for people who otherwise could not afford a lawyer.

Other Legal Opportunities!

There are many, many ways that you can work within the legal profession. Here are just a few ideas:

A *corporate lawyer* practices preventative law — he or she hopes to avoid time-consuming and expensive lawsuits.

Public defenders represent people accused of committing serious crimes who can not afford to pay for a lawyer.

Judges come in many flavors. They may be appointed or elected. Most judges are lawyers. They may serve in special courts such as traffic court or juvenile court.

Court clerks keep records of legal cases and help judges in the courtroom.

Legal aids or *paralegals* assist lawyers in private practice and in public programs which are designed to help poor people with their legal concerns.

Legislators are elected by the people. They do not have to be lawyers but often are.

Lobbyists are either lawyers or are very familiar with the law. They work to get the ideas of their special interest groups (such as banks, farmers, etc.) heard by legislators.

Legal secretaries help prepare and proof all the many long documents it seems to take to practice law.

A *notary* or *notary public* may take oaths or witness that the signature of a person on a document was truly written by that person.

ALL THE BEST! A Glossary of Plain English Legal Terms

Accessory: Not a tie or a scarf, but a person who helps commit a crime, even if they were not present, such as planning the crime or driving the getaway car. The law considers you just as guilty as the person who actually committed the crime. Being an accessory is a good way to tie yourself up in legal knots!

Affidavit: A written statement you swear to be the truth.

Aid & Abet: To knowingly participate in the commission of a crime.

Alibi: Proof that someone was not at the scene of a crime. (And you thought it was hard to get Mom to believe your story? Just try the judge!)

Appeal: Protesting the verdict of a trial and taking the case back to court for another try.

Arraignment: A formal hearing where a person is charged with a crime.

Bar: Not a place to drink, but the licensed legal profession.

Brief: A short, written statement of legal information.

Burden of Proof: The requirement to show evidence of guilt in a trial.

Capital Punishment: Not trying to find a parking place near the courthouse, but the legal killing of a person convicted of a crime.

Civil Trials: Trials related to money, insurance, and other such matters. People don't always act civil at a civil trial.

Criminal Trials: Trials related to robbery, murder, and similar crimes.

Damages: Not what happens when you kick a soccer ball through the window, but money awarded to a person as a result of a trial.

Decision: The finding, or decision, of the court in a legal matter.

Default: The failure to do what the law requires. If you don't obey the law, its "default" of nobody but yourself!

Double Jeopardy: A person cannot be tried twice for the same crime. Does that mean that even if you were guilty, but found innocent, that you couldn't be tried again? Yes. Yes.

Due Process: The guarantee that a person accused of a crime will receive a fair trial.

Felony: A serious crime, such as murder.

Indictment: Being formally accused of a crime.

Jurisdiction: The area of the law that a court has control over.

Justice of the Peace: A person who can perform simple legal tasks, such as marrying a couple.

Legal Signature: A person's real name (or mark, such as X, if they cannot write). What is your legal signature?

Liability: Responsibility.

Libel: Writing false things about another person.

Misdemeanor: A minor crime.

Murder: There are all kinds of murders. In the "first degree" means you planned it ahead of time. "Second degree" murder means you were mad but didn't intend to kill someone. Murder in the "third degree" means you accidentally killed.

Plea Bargain: When lawyers get together and decide that the person accused of a crime can go free or get a shorter sentence IF they will give information that may be damaging to them, but help put other criminals in jail.

Power of Attorney: When you let another person legally act on your behalf.

Reasonable Doubt: In a trial, a person's guilt must be proved beyond a "reasonable doubt."

Sentence: The punishment a person found guilty of a crime is given.

Slander: Saying false things about another person.

Statue of Limitations: The limit of time in which a crime must be tried.

Subpoena: A piece of paper that orders you to appear in court.

Tort: A wrongful action by one person against another.

Ward of the Court: A person, such as a young child, who may be represented by the court because they can't represent themself.

Will: A written document stating what you want to happen to your body and your possessions after your death.

Youthful Offender: A young person who has committed a less serious crime. The court tries to help the person so that this will be their first, and last!, time on the wrong side of the law.

A Glossary of Foreign Legal Terms, in Plain English!

Amicus Curiae: Latin; a "friend of the court."

Bona Fide: Latin; means "in good faith", or without any fraud or deception.

Caveat Emptor: Latin; "let the buyer beware", or, you should pay attention to what you purchase!

Certiorari: Latin; a writ or legal document.

Corpus Delicti: Latin; the proof that a crime has actually been committed.

De Facto: Latin; something that actually exists or is a fact.

De Jure: Latin; lawful.

Habeus Corpus: Latin for "produce the body"; in other words, either show reason to keep a person accused of a crime in jail, or let them go.

Ipso Facto: Latin; "by the fact itself."

Nolo Contendere: Latin; when an accused person says that they do not wish to argue that they are not guilty of a crime.

Prima Facie: Latin; "At first sight"; meaning that on the face of it, evidence appears to be true.

Voir Dire: A French term that means "to speak the truth"; this is when potential jurors are questioned about their knowledge about a crime and their feelings about such matters.

Bibliography

BOOKS

Virginia Government for Kids: The Cornerstone of Everyday Life in Our State!
by Carole Marsh/Gallopade Publishing Group

Beyond a Reasonable Doubt: Inside the American Jury System
by Melvyn Bernard Zerman/Thomas Y. Crowell, New York

Careers in the Legal Profession
by Elinor Porter Swiger/Franklin Watts, New York

Democracy, An Owner's Manual
Published by Vote USA, Washington, DC

Old Time Punishments
by William Andrews/Dorset Press, New York

You Can't Eat Peanuts in Church & Other Little-Known Laws
by Barbara Seuling/Doubleday, New York

ONLINE

Supreme Court, decisions and biographies
http://www.law.cornell.edu/supct

U.S. Congress
Send e-mail to congress @hr.House.Gov

VIDEO

Brown Vs. The Board of Education, 19 minutes, Coronet, Deerfield, IL

CD-ROM

Virginia Facts & Factivities, Carole Marsh Family CD-ROM, Gallopade Publishing Group

About the Author

Carole Marsh is the author of more than 10,000 book for young readers. She began her writing career in high school and has been writing ever since. The author started out writing mysteries based on real historic sites; she used her children and their friends as characters in these stories.

Writing fiction based on reality led her to write non-fiction. She wrote books on Shakespeare, chess, Latin and many other subjects. Young readers enjoyed her conversational tone and sense of humor.

Because her books were so popular, she was asked to write a trivia book about her home state of North Carolina that would be "less boring than a textbook." The trivia book she wrote was so well-received, that she then wrote a similar book for all 49 other states!

Today, her mystery character children are grown up, but they work as professionals alongside their mother, helping to produce, manufacture, and market her many titles. The family business is also involved in multimedia and online products.

Will Carole Marsh ever run out of ideas for books for children? "Not as long as teachers, librarians, parents, and kids continue to make such great suggestions!" she says.

Does the author worry that her readers will infringe on her *legal copyrights*? "Not a bit!" says the author. "Teachers and librarians are good 'keepers of the law;' they want students to understand that the words they write are all a writer owns to make a living." Besides, Marsh generously gives teachers permission to copy activity pages in her books for students in the class.

"It's not against the law if you have *permission*," the author reminds students. "Writing is about sharing."

Special Index

ACTIVITIES, 7, 9, 11, 12, 13, 15, 17, 21-25, 27
Virginia law, 6
Virginia Supreme Court, 20
Attorneys, 20
Breaking the law, 16
Changes in laws, 8
Children and the law, 18
Children's rights, 19
Citizenship, 15
Common law, 6
Courts, 20
Criminal Law, 20
Everyday law, 9
How laws are passed, 14
Improvements in the law, 13
Jury, 20, 22
Lawyers, 20
Legal careers, 28-29
Law people, 20
Legal precedents, 7
Legal process, 5
Legal resources, 34
Legal terms, 25, 30-33
Legal trivia, 26
Legislation, 7
Legislature, 11
Local laws, 12
Miranda, 26
Morals and ethics, 27
Old Time Punishments, 17
Reasons for laws, 8
Silly laws, 10
Trial of the century, 20-25
Types of law, 5, 7